Inspiring
Women
Every Day

March
A HEALTHY SENSE OF SELF
····························
CLAIRE MUSTERS

April
REASONS TO REJOICE
····························
EMS HANCOCK

Plus… Special Article, Ministry Report and CWR Events Page

MIX
Paper from
responsible sources
FSC® C015900

CLAIRE MUSTERS

Claire Musters is a freelance writer and editor, mum to two young children, pastor's wife, worship leader and school governor. Claire's desire is to help others draw closer to God through her writing, which focuses on marriage, parenting, worship, discipleship and issues facing women today.

EMS HANCOCK

Ems Hancock is a speaker and author based in south Manchester. She and her husband Jon have four children and are part of the Ivy network of churches. Ems runs a monthly women's lunch and is a regular speaker at churches, conferences and events. Find out more and access her blog at emshancock.com

Copyright © CWR 2016. Published by CWR, Waverley Abbey House, Waverley Lane, Farnham, Surrey GU9 8EP, UK. Tel: 01252 784700 Email: mail@cwr.org.uk
Registered Charity No. 294387. Registered Limited Company No. 1990308.
Front cover image: Stocksy/ Aleksandra Jankovic
Concept development, editing, design and production by CWR. Printed in England by Linney Print.
Unless otherwise indicated, all Scripture references are from the Holy Bible, New International Version® Anglicised, NIV® Copyright © 1979, 1984, 2011 by Biblica, Inc.® Used by permission. All rights reserved worldwide.

A Healthy Sense of Self

Looking at the **heart**

1 Samuel 16:1–13

'People look at the outward appearance, but the LORD looks at the heart' (v7)

I n our self-centred culture, it can be easy, even for us as Christians, to get caught up in focusing on ourselves. Be reassured that this month's notes won't be like that, but will be a reminder to live out of a sense of who we *truly* are – and what that really means day by day. Too often we can find ourselves living out of a warped sense of self and struggling with our identity when, ultimately, it can only be found in Jesus.

Part of stepping into who we are is learning to walk into the freedom already won for us, but the other part is about discipline and – with the help of the Holy Spirit – choosing to embrace our God-given identity every day.

So where does our sense of self come from? Does it come from what we do or achieve? Does it come from what others think of us, or what we think of ourselves? How do we measure ourselves? Is our first port of call to go to God and His Word to see what He says about us – or do we rely on what society is telling us and what it says we should be like?

I love the reminder that today's passage gives us: God looks at the *heart*. Samuel's expectation of what the next king of Israel would *look* like meant that he needed reminding that what is most important is what is going on *inside* a person – not their outer appearance. As we start a month's study on 'self', let's not forget that the way we judge ourselves is so often different to the way God judges us. He is most concerned about our spiritual wellbeing, and for us to come into the fullness of what it means to be 'new creations' in Jesus.

For prayer and reflection

Thank You, Lord, that I need only look to You to understand who I truly am. Help me, through the coming days, to learn to see myself as You see me. Amen.

Made in **His image**

Psalm 139:1–16

'I praise you because I am fearfully and wonderfully made' (v14)

So many of us can have trouble accepting ourselves for who we are – our bodies in particular come under such scrutiny, often because of the thousands of unhelpful messages and impossible standards we are bombarded with by society (through advertising, social media etc). We need to stop and remind ourselves regularly that we have been created by God – Genesis tells us that we are actually made in His image (1:26)!

I find this psalm so comforting – but also challenging. God is always close; surrounding us at all times. But how often do we forget, when worried about how we look, that God formed us in our mothers' wombs and knew *exactly* what we would be like. I said yesterday that God is most concerned with inner rather than outer appearance – and yet He *still* took the time to lovingly put our bodies together. If you have ever spent any time looking in detail at the biology of the human body, it is nothing short of miraculous. Take our DNA, for example. If all the cells in your body were uncoiled, they would stretch about 10 *billion* miles! (In other words, they would make it to the moon and back something like six thousand times.) God's design for humans is mind-blowing!

For prayer and reflection

We are going to spend some time over the next few days looking at who God says we are, and how those truths should be feeding our sense of self. But first, let's grasp the amazing truth that God – the Creator of the universe – also chose, before the creation of the world, to create you and me. Isn't that incredible?

Sorry, Lord, that I can spend time fixating on the parts of my body that I don't like rather than thanking You for creating me. I *am* 'wonderfully made'! Amen.

Children of God

Yesterday we looked at how God created not only the universe, but us, too – and He took great care with each individual. It is important to remember that He is behind all our natural talents and gifts as well. Before we start to look at ourselves and begin to feel even a whiff of pride, we should remember that without God 'nothing was made that has been made' (John 1:3). Everything in creation is down to Him – us included. The basis for our sense of self, therefore, should be rooted only in Him. Yes, we are each valuable and unique – but only in and through Him. I find that comforting, and it takes away the need for us to compare ourselves with others (something I can easily fall into doing).

Before the creation of time, God's plan for salvation was at work, too – to send Jesus, 'the true light' (v9), into the world. With His sacrifice, and our belief in Him, we have the right to call ourselves children of God; faith in His saving grace is all it takes to be adopted into His family. If you have never asked Jesus to forgive your sins, dwell in your heart and change you from the inside out to be more like Him, I urge you to do so today. And, if you have, remind yourself that however you feel about yourself right now, and however you are treated by those around you, you *are* a child of the living God, the most powerful and loving being in the universe. How privileged you are to be able to call yourself His child! Here is how John puts it in 1 John 3:1: 'See what great love the Father has lavished on us, that we should be called children of God! And that is what we are!'

John 1:9–13

'Yet to all who did receive him, to those who believed in his name, he gave the right to become children of God' (v12)

For prayer and reflection

Lord, I thank You that everything I am is because of You. Since believing in You, I have been adopted into Your family and can call myself Your child. Amen!

WEEKEND

Precious to Him

For reflection: Isaiah 43:1–7

'you are precious and honoured in my sight' (v4)

This weekend, let's take some time to pause and remember just how precious we are to God.

Many scriptures speak of His great love for us, but one that I come back to time and time again is Isaiah 43. In moments of stress, fear and weariness it is wonderful to be able to read in God's Word: 'Do not fear, for I have redeemed you; I have summoned you by name; you are mine' (v1). That works on my soul like a soothing balm. I know it is important not to take verses out of context – and this chapter was written to Israel while captive in Babylon to reassure them of His restoration. However, God's Word is 'alive and active' (Heb. 4:12) and has much to say to us corporately and individually today. So this reassures me of the high regard God has for me.

You might find it helpful to spend some time looking up Bible verses that speak to you about how much God loves you. Here's one more to get you started, which you could use as a prayer: 'keep me as the apple of your eye' (Psa. 17:8). Keep them in a journal and refer back to them regularly. You are precious to Him!

Optional further reading

For a great list of Bible verses on identity, visit www.ficm.org and search, 'Who I am in Christ'.

Worthy of His love

Our society is always pushing us to do more, achieve more, be more – and listening to these messages can erode our sense of self-worth. I know that struggling with low self-esteem is hugely difficult, and I certainly don't want to belittle what some of you may have been through as a result. My intention in writing on this subject is to encourage each one of us with a reminder of who God says we are. In order to counteract the negative pressure of the world, we need to continually soak ourselves in truth. So this next week's readings centre around who God says we are – and why.

We begin by reminding ourselves of something we touched on last week: God chose us to be His 'before the creation of the world'. We aren't worthy in and of ourselves, but because God chose to make us 'holy and blameless in his sight' through the sacrifice of Jesus. Why did God do this? Verse 5 gives us the answer: 'in accordance with his pleasure and will'. Just let that truth soak into you: you are worthy of His love through Jesus, and it gives God great pleasure to love you!

I know that the Church can have a tendency to be affected by the culture around it, and that some are concerned that as westernised Christians we are becoming too 'I'-centred. But knowing our worth as it is found in Jesus – and learning to love ourselves as God loves us – isn't a selfish thing. In Matthew 22:39 Jesus says that each one of us should, 'Love your neighbour as yourself'. If we're going to do a good job of loving our neighbours, we need first to learn to accept the worth that God gives to us.

Ephesians 1:3–8

'In love he predestined us for adoption' (vv4–5)

For prayer and reflection

Thank You, Lord, for the reminder that You find me worthy of Your love – and that I am to love myself too. Help me to do that today. Amen.

New creations!

2 Corinthians 5:16–21

'if anyone is in Christ, the new creation has come: the old has gone, the new is here!' (v17)

We start today with the amazing truth that we are new creations in Christ. There may be things we are ashamed of from our past, but God is saying that it is time to let go. Once we have asked for forgiveness, 'he is faithful and just and will forgive us our sins and purify us from all unrighteousness' (1 John 1:9). He has made us new creations, from the inside out. In our hearts He has placed His light, which reorders everything – our beliefs, feelings, actions, wills.

This includes a new perspective on others, which is why Paul instructs the disciples to 'regard no one from a worldly point of view' (v1). Wow – that's certainly a challenge right there, isn't it? But, as we shall explore further tomorrow, God has changed us for a reason – to be His ambassadors. We are to be made into the righteousness of Christ in order to reconcile others to Him too.

Isaiah 61:10 (more on Isaiah next month) reminds us that being clothed in righteousness is a reason to rejoice in God! 'I delight greatly in the Lord; my soul rejoices in my God. For he has clothed me with garments of salvation and arrayed me in a robe of his righteousness'. Just think about the trade that God did in order for us to be righteous: our worthless, ugly sin for His righteousness, which is of immeasurable worth. In the parable of the pearl of great price (Matt. 13:45–46), Jesus said that the kingdom of heaven is like a merchant looking for a great pearl – when he found it he was willing to give up everything else in order to buy it. That is how great a treasure it is for us to become new creations in Christ.

For prayer and reflection

Lord, may I never lose the wonder of how You transformed me from wretched sinner to beloved daughter. Today I choose to delight in being a new creation. Amen.

CWR MINISTRY EVENTS

DATE	EVENT	PLACE	PRESENTER(S)
3-5 Mar	Bible Discovery Weekend: Behold the Man	Waverley Abbey House	Philip Greenslade
9 Mar	Meeting Pastoral Care Challenges	WAH	Andy Peck
16 Mar	The Life and Times of Jesus	WAH	Andy Peck
21 Mar	Inspiring Women Spring Day: Living Wholeheartedly	WAH	Paula Buchel and the Inspiring Women team
23 Mar	Small Group Essentials	WAH	Andy Peck
24-26 Mar	Inspiring Women Spring Weekend: New Beginnings	WAH	Paula Buchel, Elizabeth Hodkinson and the Inspiring Women team
25 Mar	Mental Health and the Church	WAH	Mick Brooks
27-31 Mar	Introduction to Biblical Care and Counselling	Pilgrim Hall	John Munt and team
29 Mar	Great Chapters of the Bible: The Master Story	WAH	Philip Greenslade
22 Apr	Waverley Abbey College Open Day	PH	Heather Churchill, John Munt and team
22 Apr	Insight into Self-Acceptance	WAH	Chris Ledger
27 Apr	Experiencing God	WAH	Andy Peck

Please pray for our students and tutors on our ongoing BA Counselling programme at Waverley Abbey College (which takes place at Waverley Abbey House and Pilgrim Hall), as well as our Certificate in Christian Counselling and MA Counselling qualifications.

We would also appreciate prayer for our ongoing ministry in Singapore and Cambodia, as well as the many regional events that we are embarking on this year.

For further information and a full list of CWR's courses, seminars and events, call +44 (0)1252 784719 or visit www.cwr.org.uk/courses

You can also download our free Prayer Track, which includes daily prayers, from www.cwr.org.uk/free-resources

Created for **His work**

Ephesians 2:1–10

'we are God's handiwork, created in Christ Jesus to do good works, which God prepared in advance for us to do.' (v10)

We have looked at how God has made us to be new creations, or 'alive with Christ' (v5). Not only that, we are 'seated with him in the heavenly realms' (v6) – we have eternal life now to enjoy and an inheritance with Jesus.

Our key verse for today shows us that we have ready-prepared 'good works' to do. Often our sense of self can unhealthily be caught up in what we do – our society seems to like labelling people by their jobs, and, as a result, one of the first questions we ask people when we meet them is, 'So, what do you do?' While it isn't healthy to find our identity solely in our jobs, God fashioned us to enjoy living purposeful lives – and that includes doing His work. It is really important that we remember, as our passage today reminds us, that our salvation is a gift of grace – *not* something we have worked to earn. Since we have been saved, however, God *does* have a particular purpose for each one of us to undertake. Isn't that exciting?

I think that we can easily fall into the trap of compartmentalising our lives, and somehow viewing what we do specifically for the church as God's work, whereas everything else is somehow outside of that remit. However, I firmly believe that God wants to be involved in every single area of our lives. Being alive with Christ means we have an active relationship with God at all times. We can be doing His good works just as much in the way we conduct ourselves at work or in front of our neighbours – even in our leisure time – and, in fact, that reveals the evidence of God being at work in our lives to those around us.

For prayer and reflection

God, I am so grateful that You have made me alive in Christ, and created me for a specific purpose. Help me to live that out each day. Amen.

Part of the **royal priesthood**

O ur sense of self-worth can be influenced by how we are treated by those around us, especially those close to us. I struggled in this area recently as some of my once close friends began to steadily disengage from me. I felt excluded from the circle of friendship as a result. Have you ever been in a similar situation? We can take great comfort from today's passage! At the start it says that Jesus was 'rejected by humans but chosen by God and precious to him' (v1). Yes, there will be moments when we are rejected – that is part of the cost of following Him – but that pales into insignificance against the fact that we are precious to God.

What can give us an extra sense of value and significance is knowing that we are part of something much bigger than ourselves – a holy nation, a royal priesthood. These phrases are first found in the Old Testament, where Israel was called God's holy nation. God taught them to 'set apart' priests to undertake the rituals and sacrifices necessary for God to dwell with them. But when Jesus came, He was the ultimate high priest. While other priests had to offer sacrifices for their sins, Jesus offered Himself as a sacrifice for all our sins – forever! In this amazing act of redemption He has made us to be priests – also 'set apart' to reflect the holiness of God to the world around us.

As we see in this passage, we are being built into a spiritual house. We remain close to Jesus, the foundation on which we are built, but are also united with other believers. We are never alone.

1 Peter 2:4–10

'you are a chosen people, a royal priesthood, a holy nation, God's special possession' (v9)

For prayer and reflection

Rather than focusing on the times when I may be rejected, I choose to thank You, Lord, for the privilege of being part of Your chosen people. Amen.

One body, many parts

1 Corinthians
12:12–27

'Now you are the
body of Christ,
and each one of
you is a part of it.'
(v27)

Today's passage continues the theme of how we are part of something much bigger than ourselves. Yes – we are significant in our own right, chosen and loved by God, but we are also part of His wider body. Even so, let's not compare ourselves to another person, and the role that they have, and think that we are less important as a result. I love the graphic picture Paul paints for us in this passage – imagine a foot saying that it can't be part of the body because it isn't a hand! And yet, so often, we can disqualify ourselves using the very same logic. Remember: God never disqualifies us.

The text also talks about honour. Let's not look down on anyone else because they are different from us, or because they have a role that we think is less than ours. Instead, let's go to great lengths in order to preserve the unity of the body of Christ. Verse 13 talks of there being no ethnic, cultural or social distinctions between us. We need to focus on what it is that unites us: our faith in Jesus Christ.

For prayer and reflection

**Lord, thank You
that I am a vital
part of Your body,
the Church. Help
me to set aside
any feelings of
jealousy or apathy
towards others
today. Amen.**

It's great to celebrate the diversity that we find in the Church. I always wonder: where else could you find a group of like-minded yet such different people, of all ages and backgrounds, who work together so well? The Church is an amazing reflection of God's grace and creativity. As individuals we should be proud and honoured to be part of God's body, and actively cultivate 'equal concern' for those in the body whom we interact with regularly. Can I challenge you to think honestly about how you respond to others in the Church a) that are being honoured and b) are suffering?

WEEKEND

Looking in the wrong places

For reflection: Jeremiah 17:5–8

'blessed is the one who trusts in the LORD, whose confidence is in him.' (v7)

This weekend, let's take some time to think about what it is that shakes our sense of self (such as unemployment or health difficulties), and to consider if there is anything else that we put our trust in regarding who we are (such as the opinion of others).

The Archbishop of Canterbury, Justin Welby, made a beautiful statement about God-given identity when talking to the press last year about his family circumstances: 'In the last month, I have discovered that my biological father is not Gavin Welby but, in fact, the late Sir Anthony Montague Browne… I know that I find who I am in Jesus Christ, not in genetics, and my identity in him never changes.'*

Reflect honestly now: could you have remained as unshaken by this news as the Archbishop? If you know there are other things that you look to to give you your identity, surrender them to God today. Remember, when we place our confidence and trust in Him we can be like 'a tree planted by the water' (v8), not fearing whatever heat or droughts may come our way.

Optional further reading

Beloved by Rachel Gardner (London: IVP, 2015)
Am I Beautiful? by Chine Mbubaegbu (Milton Keynes: Authentic Media, 2013)

*Read the full article at www.archbishopofcanterbury.org

MON **MAR 13**

Taking off and putting on

Colossians 3:1–14

'since you have taken off your old self with its practices and have put on the new self' (vv9–10)

We have spent some time understanding that we are accepted and loved by God as His children. However, this passage instructs us that, because we have now been 'raised with Christ', there is a mandate to: 'Set your minds on things above, not on earthly things' (v3). There is a process in our journey with God, and part of that means learning to 'take off' our old, sinful self, and 'put on' the new self we have in Him. I love how direct these verses (in a similar passage) in Ephesians are about this: 'You were taught, with regard to your former way of life, to put off your old self... and to put on the new self, created to be like God in true righteousness and holiness' (Eph. 4:22–24).

I find the active imagery extremely useful here. While we know we are new creations in Christ, we can have a tendency to slip back into the clothing from our old nature, but we are reminded to purposefully clothe ourselves with the virtues of our new nature. In the church I attend, we recently had a word from God, telling us to stop putting our old, filthy rags back on as He has provided each one of us with a dazzling white garment. While we may find that old clothing comfortable and 'easy' to wear, it is actually dirty and unhealthy for us.

I find it really challenging to think about these characteristics as if they are clothing. We take care deciding what to wear each day – but do we take the same amount of care and consideration over clothing ourselves in kindness, gentleness and patience each day, for example? Take some time to think about this today.

For prayer and reflection

I am sorry, Lord, when I choose to wear clothing from my earthly nature. Teach me instead how to actively 'put on' my new self, daily. Amen.

Getting rid of **selfishness**

Philippians 2:1–11

'Do nothing out of selfish ambition or vain conceit.' (v3)

One of the characteristics of our earthly nature is selfishness. I love this quote by Jerry Bridges, as it recognises that selfishness is our default setting, but also that we can learn to put off such habits: 'It is our habit to live for ourselves and not for God. When we become Christians, we do not drop all this overnight. In fact, we will spend the rest of our lives putting off these habits and putting on habits of holiness.'* I find that really encouraging – we are *all* on a journey, and it takes time – so we need to remember not to condemn ourselves when we don't always get things right.

If we are honest, it can be really difficult to value others above ourselves and to look out for their needs more than our own. That's almost an upside-down way of living, isn't it – but often that is what God's 'kingdom living' looks like. In those moments when we feel the demands are too high, we are told to look to Jesus' example. Verses 6–11 focus on His selflessness while here on earth – and how God rewarded Him.

I find verse 6 particularly challenging; if we feel trying to be less selfish is beyond us, let's remember that Jesus 'did not consider equality with God something to be used to his own advantage'. If the One who was truly equal with God was willing to humble Himself and be obedient, shouldn't that be sufficient motivation for us to follow suit? Don't get me wrong – I know that this can be a battle every day, but I think this passage helps us to soberly put things in perspective. It's about learning to lay down our rights in order to serve others.

For prayer and reflection

Lord Jesus, I am humbled once more when I think about how You laid down Your rights and were willing to sacrifice Yourself – for me. Amen.

*Jerry Bridges, *The Pursuit of Holiness* (Cumbria: Alpha, 1999)

Self-seeking attitudes

Romans 2:1–11

'But for those who are self-seeking and who reject the truth and follow evil, there will be wrath and anger.' (v8)

Our passage today invites sober reflection: those who choose to be self-seeking will incur God's wrath and anger. The book of Romans is written as a letter to the church in Rome and, in the previous chapter, Paul describes the practices of sinful people. The church may have been feeling smug at this point. In chapter 2, however, he tells the church not to judge others, making it very clear that it is only through Jesus' sacrifice that we can be made right before God. The good news is that by choosing to accept Jesus as Lord, we no longer 'reject the truth'. We can, of course, still have a tendency to slip back into our old ways – which is why I think we need to learn to be more self-aware.

One of the elders at my church recently mentioned in a sermon that God had been revealing to him how self-centred he could be. It was brave of him to be so truthful, and hugely encouraging for the listening congregation. We can all have a tendency to want to hide our faults from others. But God wants us to live together in community, encouraging one another towards holiness – and part of that is through being honest about our struggles.

Often, it is as we draw closer to God that He begins to point out those things that He wants to change in our character (things we perhaps haven't seen). It is really helpful to ask God, and close friends too, to show us anything they feel could be a blind spot in our lives, so that we learn to be more self-aware about where we are at any given moment – and what God wants us to actively 'take off'.

For prayer and reflection

Are there any particular areas of your life in which you know you can be self-seeking? Bring these to God and ask Him to change your perspective.

Add your voice
to the prayers for transformation

As a reader of *Inspiring Women Every Day*, you are already supporting the wider ministry of CWR. Thank you!

Today, we would love to invite you to join with us further through prayer and partnership.

> *'sisters, pray for us that the message of the Lord may spread rapidly and be honoured, just as it was with you.'*
> 2 Thessalonians 3:1

CWR's ministry started out by providing people with devotional thoughts and asking them to pray for world revival. Today, our focus is to help people apply God's Word to their daily life and encourage personal transformation.

From resourcing parent and toddler groups to sending inspirational books to prisons, we are involved in many different areas of Christian life – and you can play a vital part. We ask that you would support us financially and pray for the ministry; that God's will would be done in all the lives we reach with His Word. To find out more about what we do, visit **www.cwr.org.uk**

Partner with us

As a Partner, you will be invited to special events to hear more about the charity and will receive regular updates on the work we are achieving together. To become a CWR Partner, call Carol on **01252 784709** or email **partners@cwr.org.uk**

Recognising **self-righteousness**

Matthew 23:1–12

'Everything they do is done for people to see' (v5)

Paul wasn't the only one to call people out – Jesus too exposed the self-righteousness of the religious leaders of His day. In their culture, such leaders were extremely respected and powerful – it seems that the power had gone to their heads and made them blind to their own faults.

Jesus wasn't suggesting that people should ignore what the religious leaders were telling them to do, but He did explain how the leaders' own lives differed from the standards they set for others. They obeyed the letter of the law in order to look good, but their hearts were far from God.

Later on in the chapter, Jesus speaks directly to them: 'Woe to you, teachers of the law and Pharisees, you hypocrites! You are like whitewashed tombs, which look beautiful on the outside but on the inside are full of the bones of the dead and everything unclean (v27).

As we noted yesterday, it can be hard to see the faults in ourselves – but Jesus reminds us how vital it is to deal with them first: 'You hypocrite, first take the plank out of your own eye, and then you will see clearly to remove the speck from your brother's eye' (Matt. 7:5).

The key is in us being humble enough to admit that we all sin – and also that, when we do, we can sometimes try to explain it away rather than confess the truth. Much of that is down to not wanting to look bad in front of others, but, when you consider that it makes us like the Pharisees, self-righteousness is definitely something to fling off!

For prayer and reflection

Lord, help me to recognise when I am falling into the trap of self-righteousness. Make me humble enough to admit when I make mistakes. Amen.

Relying on ourselves

aul wrote his letter to the Galatian church because he could see how they were being seduced by false teachers, who were emphasising the need to follow the letter of the law – that Gentiles had to become Jews in order to be saved. But Paul makes a point of reminding them that it is faith that saves (using the example of Abraham and his children). He goes on to explore how those who rely on the law to save them only end up being condemned.

I think this passage highlights a trait that can still be found among Christians today. We may accept Jesus' salvation through the gift of faith (which is given to us by the Holy Spirit), but then try to work hard for that very same salvation through what we do for God after we are saved. It's as if we originally believed Jesus can save us, but, since then, have fallen back into relying on ourselves. We need to be aware of this trap, as it is one that can be dangled in front of us – and it looks so respectable and plausible. Yes, it is important that we undertake to read God's Word and talk to Him daily, but, while those habits help us to grow in our understanding of God and also in the process of becoming more holy, they are not the *means* of our salvation. We need to rely on the Holy Spirit's guidance and direction, rather than our own efforts – as we are so much less reliable!

It is so freeing to know that there is *nothing* we can do to earn our salvation. We can be free to be ourselves and learn to bask in the amazing transforming power of the Holy Spirit in our lives.

Galatians 3:1–14

'After beginning by means of the Spirit, are you now trying to finish by means of the flesh?' (v3)

For prayer and reflection

Thank You, Lord, for the reminder not to rely on myself. I admit that I am unreliable compared to You, so I invite Your Holy Spirit into my life afresh to guide me. Amen.

WEEKEND

Too lowly a self-image

For reflection: Exodus 3:1–20

'But Moses said to God, "Who am I that I should go to Pharaoh and bring the Israelites out of Egypt?"' (v11)

Not relying on ourselves does not mean that we should put ourselves down. The good news is that even if we think we are nobodies, the Bible shows us that God has a habit of using nobodies!

Our reading today focuses on just one chapter of Moses meeting God, but Moses responds to God's commissioning with a whole host of questions and arguments. He finally admits the reason why he does not want to be God's spokesperson: 'I have never been eloquent, neither in the past nor since you have spoken to your servant. I am slow of speech and tongue' (Exod. 4:10). God was extremely patient with him, but didn't allow Moses' calling to be put off by the low view Moses had of himself. The same is true of Gideon, whom God used mightily despite his plea: 'How can I save Israel? My clan is the weakest in Manasseh, and I am the least in my family' (Judg. 6:15).

However we may view ourselves, God is at work *in* us and reveals His glory *through* us. Meditate on this promise today: 'My grace is sufficient for you, for my power is made perfect in weakness' (2 Cor. 12:9).

Optional further reading
Exodus 4; Judges 6–7; 2 Corinthians 12:1–10

A lack of **self-control**

P aul doesn't pull any punches here. Describing what people will be like in the 'end times' (between Jesus' resurrection and second coming), a lot of it rings true for today's society. The aim of many is to continually seek after pleasure and more money – but here Paul criticises self-gratifying behaviour.

Interestingly, a lack of self-control is up there in his description. The Old Testament also talks about those who lack self-control: 'Like a city whose walls are broken through is a person who lacks self-control' (Prov. 25:28). There is a sense that being able to keep our 'self' in control is a godly character trait; indeed, as we will see tomorrow, self-control is listed as one of the fruits of the Spirit.

In verses 8–9, Paul talks about the magicians who counterfeited Moses' miracles (see Exod. 7). He was saying that, just like them, the false teachers of the day would be exposed for who they truly were. The same is true for anyone: while we may be able to hide our shortcomings from others for a while, God sees and knows who we really are. When put into stressful situations that 'squeeze' us, what is revealed? Have we learned to cultivate the kind of qualities Paul did throughout the pressures of his life (see vv10–11), or do we lose control in the face of difficulties?

I love Paul's reminder that: 'All Scripture is God-breathed and is useful for teaching, rebuking, correcting and training in righteousness' (v16). In an age when the message of the Bible is constantly being questioned, it is refreshing to be reminded that actually, it contains everything we need.

2 Timothy 3:1–17

'People will be lovers of themselves, lovers of money… proud … without love… without self-control' (vv2–3)

For prayer and reflection

Lord, I am humbled by Paul's words. I want to be known as someone who has self-control, rather than one who lacks it. Please grow this fruit in me today. Amen.

Living **by the Spirit**

**Galatians
5:13–26**

'the fruit of the
Spirit is love,
joy, peace,
forbearance,
kindness,
goodness,
faithfulness,
gentleness and self-
control' (vv22–23)

We have spent some time looking at the things that we need to actively 'take off', and yesterday saw how a lack of self-control affects our whole being. Today's passage puts in stark contrast living for our fleshy selves with living by the Spirit. We are reminded at the start that we are 'called to be free', but the only way to do this is to 'live by the Spirit'. What does this mean? Well, verses 22–26 give us a very clear indication.

If you are anything like me, you may read the list of the fruit of the Spirit and feel pretty fruitless, or perhaps 'lacking' in certain areas. Personally, I know that gentleness is not my strong point! Many years ago, a visiting church speaker challenged us to take turns thanking God for the qualities that we saw in each other. When it was suggested that I was naturally gentle, my friends fell about laughing! No – it is not a natural quality in me.

But this fruit is not something we can grow in our own strength – the Holy Spirit works in our hearts to cultivate it. As we give Him access to the whole of our hearts, His fruit will naturally grow. That is why Paul urges us to, 'keep in step with the Spirit' (v25). Our old, sinful selves have been crucified with Christ, but Paul recognises that they have desires that do assert themselves. That is when we have a choice: either we give in to what we know are unhealthy desires, or we say no to them and ask for the Holy Spirit to help us walk into the life He has called us to – one of great fulfilment and love.

**For prayer and
reflection**

**Holy Spirit, I thank
You that You grow
Your fruit within
my heart. Help
me to walk in step
with You, allowing
You access to
the whole of me.
Amen.**

The **denying** of self

W
e have already said that much of our society is selfish – people's lives are centred on getting the best for themselves. But that is not Jesus' way. We are looking at the subject of 'self', but in our reading today He says that we must deny ourselves and be willing to lose our lives! That can seem really harsh to our eyes and ears, but let's unpack it. We have seen how Jesus actually gives us a new identity when we choose to follow Him – and it is one with a rich inheritance. Nothing can compare to that. He also teaches us to love ourselves – as we need to in order to love others well.

I think what Jesus is saying here is that we need to shift our perspective. Life isn't all about trying to hang onto everything we can. As He says in verse 36, 'What good is it for someone to gain the whole world, yet forfeit their soul?' It is about making the choice not to be self-serving, but to view our lives appropriately and ensure we are willing to sacrifice everything. Sometimes we will be called to suffer – Jesus talks about taking up our cross – but we know that ultimately we have everything in the One who gave the once-and-for-all sacrifice. We have a call to a better life – but it means losing the old one.

As Phil Moore says, 'The Gospel is free, but it is not cheap.'* We find our true selves when we are willing to give up our rights to live just for ourselves. Some may pressurise or taunt us because we are Christians, but, ultimately, we are to take up our cross knowing that we will one day enjoy eternity with Jesus.

....

Mark 8:34–38

....

'Whoever wants to be my disciple must deny themselves and take up their cross and follow me.'
(v34)

....

For prayer and reflection

....

Lord, today I want to re-affirm that I am willing to give myself to You completely – whatever the cost. Thank You that You give me true life in return. Amen.

*Phil Moore, *Straight to the Heart of Revelation* (Oxford: Monarch, 2010)

Free to be **disciplined**

**1 Corinthians
9:19–27**

'Run in such a way
as to get the prize.'
(v24)

A
lthough we acknowledge that we can do nothing without God's help, we do have a choice as to how we live out our Christian lives. As our salvation does not depend on works, we *could* simply sit back and do nothing – after all, it wouldn't change how much God loves us.

However, Paul is a great example to emulate. He encourages us that being free in Christ provides us with a great opportunity to train ourselves. He uses the analogy of runners and other competitors – they put their all into their training, running hard after the prize. Being with Jesus for all eternity is our prize – isn't that worth disciplining ourselves for? If we know we struggle in certain areas, perhaps self-image or gossiping, we can put certain disciplines in place and ask for others to support us, in order to work through those issues. Paul talks about making his body a slave – he does not want to be mastered by anything other than his God and so is going all out to ensure that doesn't happen. While we are free, we are not free to indulge our earthly passions (see Gal. 5:13; 1 Pet. 2:16). The Christian life requires hard work and discipline.

I find it fascinating that Paul also says, 'Though I am free and belong to no one, I have made myself a slave to everyone, to win as many as possible' (v19). While we don't *have* to do anything to earn our salvation, God's means of reaching the world with His good news is us. Paul talks about how he makes himself amiable to all types of people so that he isn't a stumbling block to them hearing the gospel. Is that something that you consciously do?

For prayer and reflection

Lord, I know that You call me to both freedom and discipline. Help me to glorify You through the way that I live my life every day. Amen.

Self-discipline and partners

2 Timothy 1:6–13

'For the Spirit God gave us does not make us timid, but gives us power, love and self-discipline.' (v7)

P aul wrote this letter to Timothy from prison, knowing that he was going to die soon. In it, he encourages Timothy to stand firm in the midst of difficulties, to 'fan into flame' (v6) the gift already inside him. It is obvious that Paul was enduring persecution for his faith, but he knew Timothy's leadership was also under fire and was reminding him that he had all he needed. All Christians, whether leaders or not, have the power, love and self-discipline that comes from the Holy Spirit. Those qualities help us to 'guard the good deposit' that we each have, in the midst of whatever suffering we may endure.

I am writing this in the lead up to a women's day I am facilitating. It is about 'praising through the pain' and I have asked three women very dear to me to speak, who have retained resolute faith through incredible suffering. However, in this lead up to the event I have experienced two attacks on my character, and I don't think this is a coincidence. Reading through these verses again is like breathing lifeblood through my veins. While it feels like the enemy has found the one thing that can undermine my sense of self and my leadership of the event, I know that I don't have to wither in response, but can be bold. I *can* stand firm in Jesus and do not need to suffer shame, even though I may endure difficulties. Standing up against hurt and pain, can I urge you: whatever you are facing today, guard your heart and mind and ask the Holy Spirit to help you draw on the power, love and self-discipline He has placed inside of you.

For prayer and reflection

Lord, You have given me all I need to stand firm today. Holy Spirit, help me to avail myself of Your power, love and self-discipline. Amen.

WEEKEND

Our High Priest knows

For reflection: Hebrews 4:12–16

'we have one who has been tempted in every way, just as we are – yet he did not sin.' (v15)

This week we have been looking at how living our lives in step with the Spirit involves self-control and self-discipline. The beginning of our passage today talks about how nothing is hidden from God so we will have to give an account to Him of our lives. That is sobering: we need to take stock and watch our thoughts and actions.

However, the good news is that Jesus also experienced life as a human and knows what temptations and difficulties *really* feel like. Hebrews 2 also reveals how He was fully human, which enabled Him to break us free from the grip of sin. In the Garden of Gethsemane, just before His trial and execution, Jesus cried out to the Father for a way not to drink the cup of suffering. And yet His final response was: 'may your will be done'. He is the source of our salvation but also faced the difficulty of suffering. How incredible that we have One we can turn to who understands what we are going through. He is our strength: we are not expected to beat ourselves into submission; rather we are to look to the One who equips us to live lives that honour Him. How freeing!

Optional further reading
Matthew 26:36–45; Hebrews 2:10–11,14–18

Discover God's story
– and how you can play a part

CWR tutor and course leader Philip Greenslade introduces the new seven-day series, Living Out of God's Story.

Tell us a bit about this exciting new course.

Knowing how to approach the Bible can feel daunting. So first, the course offers a concise summary of God's saving story, tracing its key covenantal stages. Second, the course encourages us to learn to live *in* the story, by understanding what it is, where it's going, how we interact with others, and how our Christian character develops as we faithfully play our part. In this way we may learn to live *out of* the story, responding wisely and biblically to the social and ethical challenges we face today.

Who would benefit from this course and what can they expect?

Anyone interested in deepening their understanding of God's Word would benefit! And anyone with an interest in biblical ethics should come along, too. People can expect to discover how we can live counter-culturally – and begin to understand our own place in God's master story.

Living Out of God's Story

Led by Philip Greenslade and Andy Peck

Wed 3, 10, 17, 24 May and 7, 14, 21 June at Waverley Abbey House

To find out more and to book, visit **www.cwr.org.uk/courses**

Helping one another

Titus 2:1–6

'teach the older women to be reverent in the way they live… Then they can urge the younger women' (vv3–5)

We start a new week with another of Paul's letters – this time to Titus. The heart behind this passage seems to me to be all about the church family functioning as a supportive network, helping one another to live righteously. The emphasis is on self-control, but there is also an urgent call for sound teaching, purity, kindness, integrity etc.

Being honest, there have been moments in which I have found comments from older women difficult to take. These were often in the context of parenting when I had very small children. I found myself thinking that collective wisdom had moved on and the women were too old-fashioned in their opinions – and it's possible that I missed out because of my attitude.

However, what still causes me to sit up and listen is when women have modelled something beautifully, and have also taken time to simply be my friend before speaking into my life. Often the subsequent teaching is done naturally – and it is that that I think Paul is referring to here. In each example, he is urging the leader or older person to first live out the way they will then instruct others to follow. As long as that happens in an organic way, rather than one person lording authority over another, I think it is a wonderful picture of unity and support within the body. Our society often feeds us the lie that only we know what is best for our own lives, and it can harden us to input from others. If only we could be humble enough to both receive and give gentle instruction in order to build one another up and help each other live lives worthy of our callings.

For prayer and reflection

I am sorry, Lord, when I dismiss what others may try to teach me. Help me to be humble and gracious, and also to recognise when You want me to help someone else. Amen.

Accepting one another

I find it a sad indictment against the Church today that there is so much infighting. Just a brief look at social media reveals many heated arguments, in which participants often angrily accuse others of not being real Christians. Tragically, the world at large can look upon so many parts of the Church and see fracture and discord rather than unity.

In Romans, Paul urges us to look to the needs of others. If we are stronger in a particular area than someone else, we should bear with them and encourage them rather than looking down on them. If we are honest, there are particular situations when this is more difficult, but our motivation is always to be the same: we never deserved Jesus' love and acceptance but He has poured it out on us in bucket loads. How, then, can we withhold our acceptance from others?

If you know you find it difficult to accept others, or if there is one person who is springing into your mind as you are reading this, be encouraged by verse 4: 'For everything that was written in the past was written to teach us, so that through the endurance taught in the Scriptures and the encouragement they provide we might have hope.'

The Bible shows us how to love and accept others; it reveals God's love for us and how Jesus was willing to be insulted for us. It shows us the disasters that occurred when different people refused to accept one another (such as Cain with Abel, Saul with David). It also shows us how God honours those who lay down their lives for others (such as Esther, and Ruth).

Romans 15:1–7

'Accept one another, then, just as Christ accepted you, in order to bring praise to God.' (v7)

For prayer and reflection

Lord, thank You for the reminder to accept those around me. Help me to share Your love today. Amen.

Everything we need

2 Peter 1:3–11

'His divine power
has given us
everything we
need for a godly
life through our
knowledge of him'
(v3)

This is one of my favourite pieces of scripture, and I often return to it. We have been reminding ourselves this month that God provides everything we need to truly be ourselves, and here we get an incredible summary of that fact! As we are beginning to draw this month's devotions to a close, I want to include these verses as an exhortation to us all. It is precisely because God has given us all we need, by allowing us to 'participate in the divine nature' (v4), that we are able to grow the qualities described here. These are qualities that enable us to be better people; more loving, and more godly. But why? 'For if you possess these qualities in increasing measure, they will keep you from being ineffective and unproductive in your knowledge of our Lord Jesus Christ. But whoever does not have them is short-sighted and blind, forgetting that they have been cleansed from their past sins' (vv8–9). I find it fascinating that we are told twice that knowledge about God is essential (vv3,8). For me, that reaffirms the importance of knowing who my God is – and who I truly am in Him. Without that knowledge, we can too easily fall for the lie that we can never be free from a particular sin or habit, or the lie that we don't deserve the salvation we have received. But, when we are secure in God and our identity, we can put off what hinders us, and working with the Holy Spirit, we can develop ourselves further so that we reflect the nature of Jesus more and more. We *can* actively pursue spiritual maturity, living out God's values in our daily lives.

**For prayer and
reflection**

**Reflect on what
your life says
about your faith.
Does it reveal
God's kingdom?
Are you growing?**

An **eternal** perspective

W e can easily place too much emphasis on our physical bodies, which Paul likens to 'jars of clay'. Each day we are getting older and our bodies are decaying as they age. That is part of the fallen nature of our world. But today's reading is a great encouragement. Despite outward appearance, we are are being renewed and have a wonderful future to look forward to. We have a promise to hold on to: 'our citizenship is in heaven... the Lord Jesus Christ... will transform our lowly bodies so that they will be like his glorious body' (Phil. 3:20–21).

We can think of this in the light of our present circumstances too. Despite what they might look like now – no matter how difficult – from an eternal perspective they will be short-lived.

Paul describes the trials and sufferings that he endured, but defiantly states: 'We are hard pressed on every side, but not crushed; perplexed, but not in despair; persecuted, but not abandoned; struck down, but not destroyed' (vv8–9). He isn't shying away from the reality, but he is stating where his ultimate hope is: 'For our light and momentary troubles are achieving for us an eternal glory that far outweighs them all' (v17). Is that how we view our difficulties?

Why not stop and think today about the areas in your life where you may be focusing too much on the present? Whether we struggle with appearances of current circumstances, let's fix our eyes on Jesus and on our eternal future with Him.

2 Corinthians 4:7–18

'Though outwardly we are wasting away, yet inwardly we are being renewed day by day.' (v16)

For prayer and reflection

Lord, appearances can be deceiving. Help me to adopt Your perspective. Amen.

Learning to be **content**

**Philippians
4:10–13**

'I have learned
to be content
whatever the
circumstances'
(v11)

**For prayer and
reflection**

**Thank You, Lord,
that You love me,
just as I am.
I choose to fix my
eyes on You today
– help me learn
to be content,
whatever the
circumstances.
Amen.**

*For further reading on the
topic of a healthy sense
of self, try *Insight into
Self-Acceptance* by Chris
Ledger and Claire Musters
(Farnham: CWR, 2016)

I think these verses are perfect for us to round off our study as they are so encouraging – and challenging. Paul is saying that he has learned the art of being content, whatever the situation. I really feel that that is a place that God wants to guide each one of us to as well. Can we truly echo Paul's heart? And what about how we feel about ourselves?

It is so important to remember that we are works in progress – yes, we are daughters of the most high King, and are redeemed and perfect in His sight, but we are also 'being transformed into his image with ever-increasing glory' (2 Cor. 3:18). There is a process involved. Are we accepting of ourselves through that process, or are we highly critical and constantly longing to be someone we are not?* God accepts us exactly as we are, while continuing to mould and shape us through the work of His Holy Spirit. If He accepts and loves us, whatever stage of our journey we are in, surely we can accept ourselves too?

Learning to be content with ourselves is a great springboard for us to then reach out to others and to embrace all that God has for us in this life. Sometimes that may entail incredible opportunities that blow our mind – at other times it may involve difficulty and suffering. Through it all we can fix 'our eyes on Jesus, the pioneer and perfecter of faith' (Heb. 12:2), who *will* sustain us with His strength throughout our lives if only we look to Him. It is through Him, and His finished work on the cross, that we can cultivate a healthy sense of knowing who we truly are. In Him we can also learn to be content in our circumstances *and* love those around us.

Teaching for life, faith and ministry

WHAT WE DO

- **Waverley Abbey College**
  Waverley Abbey College is leading the way in Christian counselling training and is the educational arm of CWR, providing short programmes and Higher Education programmes in the area of Christian counselling.

- **CWR Courses, Seminars and Events**
  Teaching for life, faith and ministry covers Bible Discovery, Life and Discipleship, Pastoral Leadership, Inspiring Women, Small Group Central and Insight Days into various life issues. Venues are Waverley Abbey House (WAH) in Surrey or Pilgrim Hall (PH) in East Sussex.

- **We Can Come to You**
  You can have CWR's renowned teaching brought to your church or small group. Choose from our popular courses and seminars or tailor-made training.

DO YOU HAVE A HEART FOR COUNSELLING?

Introduction to Biblical Care and Counselling (IBCC)

This five-day core CWR course teaches basic counselling principles within a Christian context. It is a foundation course designed for anyone who wants to learn about themselves and how to help others effectively, no matter the level of previous knowledge and experience they have. This course is reflective, interactive and personal, using practical methods and theory.

Excellent as a stand-alone course, but also an ideal opportunity to find out if a counselling programme with Waverley Abbey College could be the next step for further training.

Dates for 2017:

Mon–Fri, 27–31 March (PH)   Mon–Fri, 26–30 June (PH)

Mon–Fri, 14–18 August (WAH)   Mon–Fri, 13–17 November (WAH)

Find out more at **www.cwr.org.uk/ibcc**

Bible Discovery

Our Bible Discovery courses are an invaluable opportunity to dig deeper into the Bible and grasp more of the wonder of God's story.

Living Out of God's Story

Led by Philip Greenslade and Andy Peck

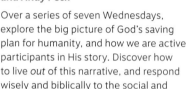

Over a series of seven Wednesdays, explore the big picture of God's saving plan for humanity, and how we are active participants in His story. Discover how to live *out* of this narrative, and respond wisely and biblically to the social and ethical challenges we face today.

Wed 3, 10, 17, 24 May and 7, 14, 21 June at Waverley Abbey House

 Also Coming Up

· **Great Chapters of the Bible:
  The Master Story – Philippians 2–3**
  Wed 29 March (WAH)

· **Hearing What God is Saying
  through the Old Testament**
  Wed 7 June (WAH)

· **Hearing What God is Saying
  through the New Testament**
  Wed 21 June (WAH)

· **Great Chapters of the Bible**
  Wed 12 July (WAH)

Insight Days

These invaluable teaching days are designed both for those who would like to come for their own benefit and for those who seek to support or understand people facing particular issues.

Insight into Self-Acceptance

Led by Chris Ledger

Come and discover how to see yourself the way God does, and positively embrace the person that God created you to be.

Sat 22 April at Waverley Abbey House

 Also Coming Up

· **Insight into Anger** Sat 12 August (WAH)

HIGHER EDUCATION PROGRAMMES IN COUNSELLING

BA (Hons) Counselling
(4/5 years part-time)
· Designed to equip students for a career in counselling by working towards professional accreditation with a professional body.*

MA Counselling
(2/3 years part-time)
· Offers study at a postgraduate level
· Designed for those with a first degree (in any subject) and a Certificate in counselling who wish to train for a professional counselling qualification.*

MA Relational Counselling and Psychotherapy
(2/3 years part-time)
· Designed for qualified therapists
· Developed to broaden skills and expertise in a number of specialist areas.

Certificate/Diploma in Counselling Supervision
(8 blocks of 2-day teaching)
· Equips students with the skills, knowledge and professional development to enable them to provide supervisory support and guidance to counsellors in clinical practice.

*Awarding accredited status is at the discretion of the professional body. As a leading educational provider in the field of Christian counselling, we are currently exploring collaboration with a new partner university commencing from September 2017.

Visit **www.waverleyabbeycollege.ac.uk** call **+44 (0)1252 784731** or email **registry@waverleyabbeycollege.ac.uk**

Waverley Abbey College

Leading the way in Christian counselling training

CWR has pioneered and developed an expertise in counselling training over the last 30 years, which is reflected in the Waverley Integrative Framework. This framework is underpinned by Christian anthropology that understands humans as created in the image of God and thus relational at the core of their being, and intrinsically valuable. Waverley Abbey College offers a range of counselling programmes to suit every level of interest in progressing and developing professional counselling skills.

 Open Days 2017

Come to one of our free Open Days to find out more. Meet the tutors, explore the campus and hear about what makes our training distinctive.

Next Open Days:

Sat 22 April (PH)

Sat 27 May (PH)

Sat 24 June (WAH)

To find out more and to book your free place, visit **www.waverleyabbeycollege.ac.uk** or call **01252 784731**.

VOCATIONAL PROGRAMME

Waverley Certificate in Christian Counselling
(1 year part-time)

- Equips students with a foundational knowledge of counselling
- Taught within and alongside Year 1 of the BA (Hons) Counselling programme
- Provides a pathway for those without formal entry qualifications to the BA (Hons) Counselling programme
- Offers an opportunity to develop vocational training in pastoral ministry.

Visit **www.waverleyabbeycollege.ac.uk** call **+44 (0)1252 784731** or email **registry@waverleyabbeycollege.ac.uk**

We Can Come To You

You can have CWR's teaching brought to your church or small group. Visit **www.cwr.org.uk/wecancometoyou** to find out more.

PICK YOUR COURSE OR SEMINAR

Christ Empowered Living

This foundational day course introduces God's original design for our personalities and how we can live well and deepen our dependence on God.

Seven Laws for Life

This dynamic three-hour seminar considers the seven key elements of a successful Christian life.

The Bible in Two Hours

Your team or small group will enjoy an eye-opening overview of the Bible, which serves as a great foundation to Bible reading.

Inspiring Women **Being a Secure Woman – in an Insecure World**

This (day, half-day or one hour) seminar unfolds the principles of becoming a secure woman in God – whatever your stage of life or circumstances.

Inspiring Women **Women Mentoring Women**

This (half-day or one hour) seminar looks at areas of ministry, work and homelife where the influence of godly women can greatly help others.

Inspiring Women **Designed for Living**

This one-day seminar looks at how to deepen our dependence on God, resolve personal problems and satisfy our deepest longings.

TAILOR-MADE TEACHING

We offer tailor-made training for: small group leaders (including topics such as leading effective discussions or Bible study); church leaders (topics such as how to preach); and for the whole church (topics such as discovering spiritual gifts).

Country Breaks and Holidays at Pilgrim Hall

Whether you are looking to enjoy some peace and quiet on your own, spend quality time with family or relax with friends, you can draw closer to God and be spiritually refreshed with a stay at Pilgrim Hall.

Dates for 2017:

- **May Country Break**
  Mon–Fri, 22–26 May

- **Summer Holiday**
  Mon–Fri, 10–14 July

- **Family Summer Holiday**
  Sat–Sat, 19–26 August

- **September Country Break**
  Mon–Fri, 28 Aug – 1 Sep

- **Autumn Break**
  Mon–Fri, 23–27 October

- **Christmas at Pilgrim Hall**
  Sat–Wed, 23–27 December

Beautiful venues for your church events

Pilgrim Hall and Waverley Abbey House are established places of retreat and refocus for churches and ministries across the country. From women's days to men's breakfasts, church leadership retreats and fun weekends for the whole church family – find out which one of our venues best suits your needs.

Pilgrim Hall

Pilgrim Hall (East Sussex)
www.pilgrimhall.com
pilgrim@cwr.org.uk
Tel: +44 (0)1825 840295

Waverley Abbey House

Waverley Abbey House (Surrey)
www.waverleyabbeyhouse.org.uk
info@waverleyabbeyhouse.org.uk
Tel: +44 (0)1252 784733

WEEKEND

The favour of the Lord

For reflection: Isaiah 61:1–11

'to proclaim the year of the LORD'S favour' (v2)

How would you react if someone told you that you would experience 'a year of God's favour'? Perhaps you would relax, not be anxious about finances or family, and breathe more deeply? Maybe for a whole year you would feel elated, calm and even joyful? It is true that God's favour and blessing gives us confidence, peace and hope. But as we journey through these verses we will find more to encourage us – God's favour also brings us a sense of calling and purpose.

This month we will take a look at the wonderful words written in Isaiah 61, a chapter entitled, 'The year of the LORD'S favour' in the NIV. If, like me, you want to unpack that more, you are in the right place! Sometimes known as the 'fifth Gospel', Isaiah gives us detailed prophetic pictures of the Messiah. Here we find a beautiful portrait of what Jesus would come to do and what impact His earthly ministry would have. As we look at these precious verses, and those that link with them from elsewhere in the Bible, let's commit to allowing God to search our hearts for places where we need to imitate Christ more and the world less.

Optional further reading
Proverbs 3:1–10; Ruth 3:13–17

Gracious words

Luke 4:18–22

'The Spirit of the
Lord is on me'
(v18)

The same wonderful words from today's reading were written in Isaiah 61 hundreds of years before Jesus was born, and yet they sum up who He was and is. I find it fascinating that this verse does not say, 'The Spirit of the Lord is *in* me', nor does it say '*with* me'. The word used for 'on' here means 'over, above and upon' – giving us the sense that Jesus was being empowered, surrounded and given authority for the task ahead. Doesn't that encourage you today? This is what we need, isn't it?

In verse 16 of today's passage, we read that Jesus went to the synagogue in Nazareth. He stood up and the scroll of the prophet Isaiah was handed to Him. Unrolling it He began to read these very words. Think for a second. Can you imagine hearing Jesus speak these verses out loud? It must have been an incredible thing to witness, especially when He ended by saying, 'Today this scripture is fulfilled in your hearing' (v21). Luke then records for us that, 'All spoke well of him and were amazed at the gracious words that came from his lips' (v22).

For prayer and reflection

As Christians we know we have the spirit of God within, but we also have His spirit *on* us. Like Jesus, we can speak words that can bless and be gracious. We can be used by God to heal and help, to nourish and guide with what we say. But do we? Do we really offer people the kind of words that leave them amazed, challenged and full of hope? Throughout the whole of this month, Isaiah's words will challenge us to imitate Christ. Today, let us be aware of who it is that empowers us and gives us our authority.

Lord Jesus, help me to remember that You are not just *with* me, but *on* me too. Help my words be gracious as a result. Amen.

Anointed and **qualified**

**Matthew
16:13–20**

'Who do people
say the Son of
Man is?' (v13)

Have you ever felt under-qualified for a role? I can remember having three children under the age of two and suddenly feeling a deep sense of panic! How could I be the kind of mother they needed? The first verse of Isaiah 61 says, 'The LORD has anointed me.' But the Amplified version of this Scripture goes further to say, 'because the LORD has anointed *and* qualified me' (emphasis added).

There are many times in life when we may find ourselves in a position where we think, 'How did I get here?' or, 'I can't do this!' Isaiah speaks of Jesus as being someone with anointing but *also* with the right qualifications. No one else could have stood in His place. No one else had His unique qualities. He was totally and utterly perfect! We know that Jesus wasn't just anointed with oil but He was anointed with a wonderful title. In fact, the Greek word *Christos* (from which we get the English word *Christ*) is the direct translation of the Hebrew word *Mashiach* or *Messiah*. This word is related to the Hebrew verb *masach*, which means 'to anoint'.

But many people – even those Jesus knew well – did not understand Him or know who He was. At one point, He asked His disciples, 'Who do people say the Son of Man is?' (Matt. 16:13). Their varying answers show their confusion.

Our anointing can also be misunderstood or hidden. There are times when we can feel as though no one understands or sees our gifts. Jesus knew what it was to be misrepresented and maligned – but that did not stop Him fulfilling His mission.

For prayer and reflection

Lord, please teach me to trust in You, even when I feel that I am under-qualified. Amen.

Good news

Isaiah 52:1–10

'How beautiful…
are the feet of
those who bring
good news' (v7)

In a world where there is so much bad news, isn't it wonderful that we have a Messiah who brings good news to us? Not just good news to those who are spiritually poor, but life-giving, joyful news for the physically poor too. Here, Isaiah shares the 'glad tidings' God's people could expect from His anointed one. Summed up in the person and purpose of Jesus is all that we need: pardon, release, restoration, hope, freedom, joy and healing. The older I get, the more I discover there is to know of Jesus' amazing purposes.

Jesus spent a great deal of His earthly ministry around those who were in need, or somehow lacking. His words and His actions constantly had the result of blessing and restoring people. Luke 1:53 tells us that He 'filled the hungry with good things'. Wherever He went, Jesus met needs of all kinds. Preaching in His actions as well as His words, every miracle was a sermon that showed us something about the kind of good news He was bringing. There is something so attractive about the gospel!

In today's key verse we read, 'How beautiful… are the feet of those who bring good news, who proclaim peace, who bring good tidings, who proclaim salvation, who say to Zion, "Your God reigns!"' This is challenging for us, isn't it? What comes out of our mouths? What are we proclaiming? How good are we at carrying that kind of good news? Do we proclaim peace and encourage others to remember that *our God reigns*? I want to be a person who changes the atmosphere with the good news of Jesus in what I do, and in what I say.

For prayer and reflection

Lord, teach me to be a person who embodies and proclaims Your good news for others. Amen.

The skilled **surgeon**

Psalm 147

'He heals the broken-hearted and binds up their wounds.' (v3)

saiah tells us a lot about the role of the Messiah in Isaiah 61:1 alone. In today's key verse we read this similarly comforting phrase, 'He heals the broken-hearted and binds up their wounds.' The Hebrew word used for 'heal' here is *raphe*, which means, 'to sew together or mend'. I have a friend who is a wonderful crochet designer. Every stitch she makes is purposeful and practised. It is there for a reason.

The phrase used for 'bind up' in both this verse and our verse in Isaiah today, comes from the Hebrew word *chabash*, which means 'to tie' or 'to bandage'.

Many of us will know what it is like to go through a traumatic time where we feel utterly broken or fragmented. These words remind us that God doesn't just want to deal with the physical wounds each of us may have. He can see what others can't and will deal with the inner pains we face too. Jesus can bind up even those wounds which are *hidden* from others – maybe in ways we are not even aware of ourselves. Every stitch He makes is purposeful too.

I don't know if you have ever had to have stitches. They are used to sew up a wound in order to hold the parts together so that they have time to heal. Isn't it wonderful that Jesus binds up the hearts of those who are struggling? He doesn't expect us to go through life with a fixed grin.

Psalm 51:17 says, 'My sacrifice, O God, is a broken spirit; a broken and contrite heart you, God, will not despise.' Jesus never fails in His surgery. His healing is effective, powerful and permanent.

For prayer and reflection

Thank You, Jesus, that You know my inner needs and that You bind me up where I am broken. Amen.

So many ways to experience the Bible every day

There is nothing more life-changing and affirming than making time for daily Bible reading and engagement with God. At CWR, we believe this wholeheartedly.

We create Bible reading resources to help people discover how accessible and relevant God's Word is today. Perhaps you know someone who would benefit from one our devotional books or daily Bible reading notes (like *Inspiring Women Every Day*)? We have resources for every age, and for different stages or aspects of the Christian life. There is much to explore!

www.cwr.org.uk

*'I just wanted to say how much I appreciated and got out of **Inspiring Women Every Day**. I felt the words written both in the Bible and in the notes were just for me. I told loads of my friends how amazing it was! Thanks for the time and effort in creating these notes.'*

Families – what about exploring the Bible together?

We are very excited to introduce our new devotional for families: *All Together: The Family Devotional.* Written by Steve and Bekah Legg, who parent a blended family with six children, this fun and accessible devotional speaks to all ages. Over 12 weeks, families can explore Bible stories, biblical truths and key characters – and draw closer to God, and each other, through His Word. Available in March.

'I've never seen one of these for families before – well done Mr and Mrs Legg!'
Jeremy Vine

Find out more at
www.cwr.org.uk/familydevotional

Our **releaser**

Psalm 18:1–6,
16–19

'he rescued
me because he
delighted in me.'
(v19)

I f you have ever felt trapped in or by a certain situation, you will know the sheer elation when that time is finally over.

In Isaiah 61:1 we are told that the Messiah came to bring freedom for captives and the 'release from darkness for the prisoners'. For those awaiting the coming of the rule and reign of God's anointed One, this was more than just a comforting – but vague – promise. The people of God had often been exiled and taken far away from what they knew. Their history documented numerous periods where they had been made to work as slaves for aggressive rulers. The Hebrews knew what it was to suffer at the hands of those who forced them to work in terrible conditions without pay. They had waited a long time for release. The coming of God's promised Messiah meant freedom from bondage, restoration of identity and release from oppression.

Today's reading speaks of this hope: 'He rescued me from my powerful enemy, from my foes, who were too strong for me. They confronted me in the day of my disaster, but the Lord was my support. He brought me out into a spacious place; he rescued me because he delighted in me' (vv17–19).

Read those verses again. Which words stand out? In what ways has God shown Himself as your rescuer and releaser? What has He saved you from?

Galatians 5:1 tells us that, 'it is for freedom that Christ has set us free'. I like to remind myself and others that this is in the present tense. It *is* for freedom. What are you doing with *your* freedom, and how are you helping others to find theirs?

For prayer and reflection

Lord, thank You that You are all about releasing and restoring. Help my life reflect that today. Amen.

WEEKEND

Jubilee

For reflection: Deuteronomy 15:12–18

'Give to them as the LORD your God has blessed you.' (v14)

Once every 50 years, the Hebrews held a special year of Jubilee (see Lev. 25), so for most people, this only happened once in a lifetime. In this wonderful life-changing year any Israelite who had been forced to sell themselves into slavery was set free, and any land that had been sold was restored to its rightful and original owners. This powerful part of the law meant that no Israelite would ever be a permanent slave, nor would any of them irrevocably lose his inheritance.

When Isaiah speaks here of the proclamation of the Lord's favour, it is said in a spirit of jubilee. The trumpet-blast of liberty announced by a shofar (an instrument made from a ram's horn) began the celebration. Matthew 24:31 is reminiscent of this. It says, 'And he will send his angels with a loud trumpet call, and they will gather his elect'. We have the ability to set people free in how we speak and act. Our lives can be examples of how God has blessed us.

In what ways can you bless others with a generous heart today? Praise God that you have been chosen to live a life of freedom where your debts have been paid.

Optional further reading

Romans 6:17–19; Jeremiah 34:8–16

God of all **comfort**

**2 Corinthians
1:3–7**

'Praise be to… the
God of all comfort,
who comforts us
in all our troubles'
(vv3–4)

Parts of Isaiah 61 read like a beautifully crafted
mission statement of promises. In verse 2,
we are shown that the Messiah is not just
someone who comforts those in distress, but someone
who will be 'Jehovah Jireh' – the God of provision – too.
Earlier in the Bible, we read that Abraham calls the hill
where God provides the ram in place of Isaac 'Jehovah
Jireh' (see Gen. 22:14). But the Greek translation of this
phrase means, 'the Lord has seen'. Isn't it wonderful
that God sees our needs and is able to meet them?
He is someone who knows the things we don't even
remember to tell Him!

In today's passage from 2 Corinthians, God is
described further as the 'Father of compassion and
the God of all comfort, who comforts us in all our
troubles, so that we can comfort those in any trouble
with the comfort we ourselves receive from God.'
I love the use of the word *all* twice here. God is not
a God of *some* comfort, but *all* comfort. Both Isaiah
and Paul are highlighting not just part of His character
but also His ability. Isn't it amazing that God *sees* our
needs and that His comfort will always exceed our
afflictions? As someone who has written extensively
on grief, I can find so much hope in these wonderful
words. Those who suffer loss will be comforted and
more than this; they will be given all they need. If you
are grieving in this season of your life, know this
truth today. It is true to say with the Gospel writers,
'blessed are those who mourn, for they will be
comforted' (Matt. 5:4).

**For prayer and
reflection**

**Jesus, thank You
that You came to
comfort us. Thank
You, too, that You
see our needs and
are able to provide
all of them. Amen.**

The God of **instead**

henever ashes are spoken of in the Bible, they are a symbol of mourning, mortality and/or the need for humbling and repentance. In 61:3, Isaiah prophesies about the most wonderful divine exchange that the Messiah will execute. I love the fact that our God is the God of 'instead'. He gives us something incredible *instead* of the awful things we so often carry. Marvellously, He also always gives us infinitely more than we can ever offer Him. God swaps our ashes for His crown, our mourning for His gladness and our ugliness for His beauty. That is the grace of God!

After a period of grief in my life, I felt as though my whole demeanour changed. I walked as though I was covered in ashes. I felt broken, lost and empty. But, little by little, God began to show me how to exchange this heaviness for His beauty. If you feel a little like this today, hear the comforting words of Jesus in Matthew 5:4–5: 'Blessed are the poor in spirit, for theirs is the kingdom of heaven. Blessed are those who mourn, for they will be comforted. Blessed are the meek, for they will inherit the earth.' This inheritance and comfort is ours in the person and purposes of Christ. He is the friend who 'sticks closer than a brother' (Prov. 18:24) and the God who sees deep down to the things we often try to hide inside.

In what ways are you holding on to 'ashes' in your life at the moment? Is there anything weighing you down or causing you to feel heavy and life-weary? Seek out a divine exchange today in a wonderful unburdening of your heart.

Matthew 5:1–10

'Blessed are the pure in heart, for they will see God.' (v8)

For prayer and reflection

Lord, I come to You with the ashes in my life, and ask You to crown me with the beauty of Your peace instead. Amen.

Joy bringer

Nehemiah 8:1–11

'Be still, for this is a holy day. Do not grieve.' (v11)

I
f you have ever been anointed with oil, you may have found it to be a memorable experience. It reminds us that we are set apart, reserved for God's purposes, marked with His spirit and power. Anointing often accompanies prayer for healing or a deep need to rid ourselves of something we're battling. Recently, I went for some prayer and was anointed with oil. I felt such inner joy as the oil touched my head and my hands. It was a physical sensation reminding me of a spiritual truth.

In Isaiah 61:3, we are told that the Messiah relieves us of mourning and bestows on us 'the oil of joy'. God wants us to know the power of His joy, even in circumstances where the *opposite* of joy is natural. At times when we are mourning, it doesn't seem possible to be joyful – but it is. Our God 'gives strength to the weary and increases the power of the weak' (Isa. 40:20). In order to understand the miracle of God's mighty strength, we first have to know what it feels like to be weary – don't we?

We read that the people in today's passage were in mourning. But Nehemiah says, 'Go and enjoy choice food and sweet drinks, and send some to those who have nothing prepared... Do not grieve, for the joy of the LORD is your strength' (v10).

I find it wonderful that God hides His strength in joy. He could have chosen to hide it in worship or prayer, or ministry – but He put it in joy.

If you feel weak today, it may be that you are in need of the oil of God's joy. In what ways do you need His joy instead of mourning in your life? Or, where do you need 'messages of joy instead of news of doom' (Isaiah 61:3, *The Message*)?

For prayer and reflection

Lord, please give me Your oil of joy today as I look at my life and the lives of those around me. Amen.

Putting on **praise**

In Bible times, a person's manner of dress reflected their mood but also their circumstances. What people wore was a clue to how they were feeling and what situation they were in.

God knows that many people are encumbered by a spirit of heaviness. A trip to a chemist will show you the amount of over-the-counter drugs that exist to help people try to combat the heaviness they are facing. We know that such medicines may help relieve symptoms, but they don't deal with the heart of the problem.

Spiritual heaviness is an *inward* issue. It is a problem so many of us face. As Charles Spurgeon wrote, 'The blessings which Jesus gives to us are not surface blessings, but they touch the centre of our being!'* When we come to know Jesus, the Holy Spirit begins to transform us from the inside out. Rather than continuing to have a character steeped in sin and despair, we receive a new nature, identifying us with the light, life and joy of Christ.

The garment of praise is adaptable, fitting anyone from the greatest spiritual achiever to the most wretched of sinners. It fits us in any and every season. Romans 13:12 says, 'so... let us cast off the works of darkness, and put on the armour of light' (ESV). There has to be a 'casting off' before a 'putting on' can occur. We can't wear the spirit of despair at the same time as the garment of praise. One must be exchanged for the other. The robe of praise is ours to wear, but we must choose to actually put it on. We need to recognise the power of praise and clothe ourselves with it. Do you need to do this afresh today?

Romans 13:8–14

'clothe yourselves with the Lord Jesus Christ' (v14)

For prayer and reflection

Lord, teach me to put on praise in exchange for heaviness. Amen.

*C.H. Spurgeon, Sermon 3349, 'The Garment of Praise', 1913

Living the Dream

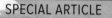

Dave Smith, Senior Pastor of KingsGate Community Church and author of *40 Days with Jesus*, *Transformed Life* and *Transformed Living*, introduces *Living the Dream*.

Living the Dream follows the story of Joseph (Exod. 37–50). Tell us, why Joseph?

The story of Joseph is a truly inspiring account. It starts with a picture of a spoilt 17-year-old from a dysfunctional family who received a dramatic dream of future greatness. Clearly unprepared to 'live the dream', he underwent a long, hard 13-year period of testing and preparation, before experiencing promotion.

For me, Joseph has been an inspiration. Saved at 19 while at university and called to start the church in Peterborough at 25, I know the power of receiving a 'dream' from the Lord, embracing His preparation, and experiencing His favour and blessing.

What is 'the dream'?

Primarily, that dream is for you to have an eternal love-relationship with God, to become His child, to be loved and to love Him for all eternity. But there is more. God has a purpose for your life that is unique to you, and He wants to reveal

it to you. Joseph lived the dream, and so can you and I. Like him, we need first to dream God's dream for our lives. As we 'see' His vision and 'hear' His word for us, we can move forward with confidence, knowing that what He has sovereignly ordained and spoken will come to pass.

What lessons do you glean from Joseph and explore in *Living the Dream*?

Like Joseph, we all have lessons to learn, such as the importance of forgiving others, using our God-given gifts and thriving even when times seem tough. You may be a young person starting out on the journey of life. If so, Joseph has much to teach you. But if, like me, you are at mid-life or entering your later years then there is still much to learn! There are new dreams to dream, new tests to pass, new blessings to experience and, of course, the promise of finishing well and leaving a great legacy. Whatever your age or whatever stage of life you are in, my prayer is that the Lord will use this book to help transform the rest of your life.

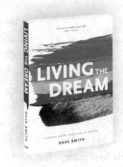

Living the Dream is available from March. To purchase, you can use the order form at the back of these notes or visit **www.cwr.org.uk/store**
ISBN: 978-1-78259-665-3

Permanent blessings

Isaiah 62:1–10

'you will be called by a new name that the mouth of the LORD will bestow.' (v2)

There is so much in a name, isn't there? A name helps people identify us from others. It allows us to call someone, speak to someone directly and refer to them. Often with Bible characters, a person's testimony or character was part of their name.

So when Isaiah speaks of those in Zion being 'called oaks of righteousness, a planting of the LORD for the display of His splendour' (Isa. 61:3), he was wanting us to know something about the significance of the oak and its reputation. In the ancient world, Romans called oak trees 'robur', from which we get the word 'robust', meaning 'strong'.

This section of Isaiah speaks of the permanence of what the Messiah had come to do. The reputation and the display of what God will do is linked to the shelter, strength and character of the oak tree. Botanists tell us that oak wood is resistant to decay and is strong and useful in many different contexts. In many ways this is what it means to be righteous.

Within the shade of oak trees was also a significant place to conduct business. In fact, a number of times in the Bible we see that courts were held, and even kings were crowned under these great trees.

God has planted the oaks for a purpose: in order to display His splendour. Perhaps today, this Good Friday, we need to remind ourselves what He has planted in us and ask ourselves what *we* are planting and displaying. Maybe we need to sit down and look over some of the things He has told us in the past and assess how far we have come. What is growing in your life right now, and is it displaying God's splendour?

For prayer and reflection

Lord, teach me how to display Your splendour and grow in a way that pleases You and draws others to You. Amen.

WEEKEND

Renew the ruins

For reflection: Isaiah 61:4–6

'They will rebuild the ancient ruins' (v4)

My husband is a man who can't walk past a piece of litter. He will quietly pick it up and put it in the nearest bin. He won't moan about the litter being there. He will simply do something about it. We live in a world where long term and short term devastation are obvious. Many of our streets are scarred by vandalism, graffiti or mess, aren't they? For us, as people of hope, it isn't enough to notice it and complain loudly to the council. We have to be people of *action*. We can actively choose to 'restore the places long devastated'. Take our friend who turned a derelict bus depot into a mobile orchard, for example. He now sells cider and apple juice from a place others had written off as 'dead space'. Or another friend, who turned a run-down warehouse site into a business enterprise for people just out of prison.

This Easter weekend, consider these questions. In what ways could you re-imagine your community and 'renew the ruined cities that have been devastated for generations'? How could you be a restorer in your neighbourhood?

Optional further reading

Isaiah 58; Joel 2:25–26

Perfect **strangers**

Isaiah 14:1–7

'How the oppressor has come to an end!' (v4)

Having strangers in charge of your property sounds a little negative doesn't it? But if we dig deeper we can see that verse 5 of Isaiah 61 is all about God *releasing* His people. Instead of being oppressed by surrounding nations, Isaiah is reminding us of the promise that God will cause other nations to *serve* Israel and bring wealth to them. One version of the Bible has an interesting translation of this scripture. It says, 'Then your *enemies* will come to care for your sheep, and their children will work in your fields and in your gardens' (Isa. 61:5, ERV, emphasis added). For the Israelite, the word 'stranger' was synonymous with the word 'enemy.' But God is speaking here of something different. This was not predicting doom and gloom, a returning into exile and slavery. This was about the Israelites having spiritual dominion, power and authority in the land. This is a reminder that God is making His people the head and not the tail (Deut. 28:13).

How often have you done an unwelcome task and thought how lovely it would be to have someone to do it for you? This is the exact feeling behind these verses. God is inviting His people to look with hope and expectation into the future when they will be wealthy enough to lead others and use people's skills to enhance their own.

Today, why don't you take some time to thank God for all those people in your life who do things for you, or on your behalf? Think about those who serve you in any way. Choose to be thankful for their part in your story.

For prayer and reflection

God, we thank You for all those who serve us and enhance our lives. We choose to name them today. Amen.

All are **priests**

A long time before Isaiah, God made a covenant with His people at Sinai where He told Moses that the Israelites were to be His 'treasured possession'. In today's passage (v6), God also says, 'Although the whole earth is mine, you will be for me a kingdom of priests and a holy nation.' So God had set apart His people, the Israelites, to serve Him in a way that was not common or usual. He was not just asking for designated priests from one tribe to serve Him. He was asking for the whole nation to identify themselves as a *kingdom* of priests and to see themselves as holy and anointed for Him.

Earlier in our study of Isaiah 61 we read that, in a spiritual sense, God was setting His people free from being oppressed by earth-bound tasks (such as working the flocks and fields). In a way, Isaiah is reminding us that when God sets us free, He sets us to work in a new way, with a fresh mindset. As believers, we are all called to be kings and priests. There is no longer a distinction between those in 'full-time ministry' and those who work 'in the world'. This theme is also picked up in 1 Peter 2:9, where we read, 'But you are a chosen people, a royal priesthood, a holy nation, God's special possession, that you may declare the praises of Him who called you out of darkness into His wonderful light.' Do you see yourself in these terms? Or do you sometimes struggle to see yourself in the way God sees you here?

Ask yourself what kind of priest God has made you. Do you see yourself as His special possession? In what way are you ministering to Him? How are you ministering to others?

Exodus 19:1–10

'out of all nations you will be my treasured possession.' (v5)

For prayer and reflection

God, thank You for calling me out of darkness into light. Help me serve You as a priest today. Amen.

WED **APR 19**

Wealth of nations

Isaiah 60:1–11

'the glory of the LORD rises upon you.' (v1)

The day I found out we were expecting our fourth baby, I admit I wondered how we would cope financially. I came home from a doctor's appointment to find a bag of clothes attached to my front door handle. I still don't know who it was from, but it contained many brand new beautiful baby clothes! It was a promise that God would continue to provide for us. It showed me that He saw my heart and my needs and was already miraculously meeting them.

Isaiah is keen to show us the deep, wide and abundant provision of God for those in His keeping. He highlights again that God's people will be in a position of favour, blessing and plenty because of *who* they serve. In verse 5 of today's passage we read, 'Then you will look and be radiant, your heart will throb and swell with joy; the wealth on the seas will be brought to you, to you the riches of the nations will come.' Can you imagine reading those verses if your family history had included lengthy spells in exile, serving foreign gods and foreign kings? The 'wealth of the seas' and the 'riches of nations' were reminders that good times were coming and that fear was unnecessary. Isaiah now promises a time of spiritual and physical reward for faithfulness: 'Your gates will always stand open, they will never be shut, day or night, so that people may bring you the wealth of the nations' (v11). This is an amazing promise.

In what ways have you seen the Lord provide for you? How has He shown Himself faithful in your everyday life? Take some time to thank Him today.

For prayer and reflection

Father, thank You for Your faithful provision. Thank You that You meet every need and hear every prayer. Amen.

Double helpings!

Job 42:10–17

'the LORD restored his fortunes' (v10)

There are six times in the Bible where we find references of people being given a 'double portion'. The earliest mention is found in Mosaic Law (Deut. 21:17). So what does it mean to receive a double portion? Rather than being a sign of greed or overeating, a double blessing is much more significant. When someone receives such a portion, they get a bigger reward – twice as much as that given to others. That person is therefore singled out, honoured, favoured and highly regarded.

So, why does God give double portions? Perhaps we can locate a clue in 1 Samuel 1:5 where we read that Hannah's husband, Elkanah, gave her a double portion 'because he loved her'. Hannah had suffered shame and grief in front of others for her lack of children. To honour her, Elkanah gives her more. We can also see this 'double for your trouble' principle at work in the story of Job. God gave twice as much to Job as he originally had before his time of great loss. 'The LORD restored the fortunes of Job when he prayed for his friends, and the LORD gave Job twice as much as he had before' (Job 42:10, Amplified). God loves to restore us. He loves to take away what we *don't* need and give us what we *do* need. But there are many times in the Bible and in our lives that we see this double blessing concept at work. We can look back and see where God gave us more than we asked for, and look ahead to 'Him who is able to do infinitely more than all we ask or imagine, according to His power that is at work within us' (Eph. 3:20). God doesn't just give us from a miserly amount, but from an abundant heart.

For prayer and reflection

Lord, thank You that You are a God of double helpings and that You give me more than enough! Amen.

Everlasting joy

Isaiah 35:1–10

'and the mute
tongue shout for
joy' (v6)

As a child, I learnt a song based on today's Scripture reading. I have found myself singing it at all sorts of times in my life. The words, adapted by Ruth Lake, are: 'Therefore the redeemed of the Lord shall return and come with singing unto Zion, and everlasting joy, shall be upon their heads...'

Everlasting joy sounds almost too good to be true, doesn't it? Many people can't imagine what consistent joy like this would feel like. We are people who go up and down with our circumstances, our finances and our problems – aren't we? But one of the promises of God is that joy can be ours – in full, and in any situation (see John 15:11).

So what does this kind of joy look like? We can sometimes confuse it with happiness, but joy like this is totally independent of our life's circumstances. It is a peaceful state of contentment driven by the belief that God is sovereign over all things.

For prayer and reflection

For me, Acts 2:28 is one of the most beautiful verses in the whole of the Bible, and gives us a clue to the reason we can know permanent joy. It says, 'You have made known to me the paths of life; you will fill me with joy in your presence.' As Christians, we know the precious presence of God with us – we are never alone. Joy is ours because of this unchanging truth. God is with us. He is for us. He is over us and He is in us.

Father, thank You that knowing You means I have access to everlasting joy. Show me where I need to grasp this. Amen.

How are your joy levels? Would you describe them as 'everlasting'? Do you feel robbed of joy because of your circumstances? Perhaps today you might need to check your heart to see if it is thriving in God's presence.

MAY/JUN 2017

May

RECOGNISING JESUS

PAMELA EVANS

June

RUNNING THE RACE

JEANETTE HENDERSON

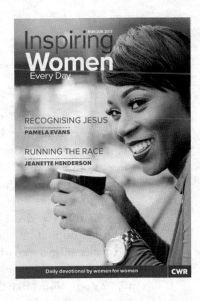

In **May**, Pamela Evans uses John's Gospel to explore who Jesus is, helping us to know Him more fully and recognise the impact He has on our lives today.

In **June**, Jeanette Henderson unpacks the apostle Paul's metaphor of running the Christian race of faith, and considers how we can press on, run well and not give up.

Obtain your copy from CWR, Christian bookshops or your National Distributor. If you would like to take out a subscription, see the order form at the back of these notes.

Also available as eBook/eSubscription

WEEKEND

Love justice

For reflection: Micah 6:1–8
'what does the LORD require of you?' (v8)

Have you asked yourself the question recently, 'What does God want of me?' It can be a tough one to answer but it is an important one to voice as often as we can. Today we are looking at one of the things God requires – justice. 'For I, the LORD, love justice' (Isa. 61:8).

Sometimes we don't love justice. You may immediately disagree with that statement, but hear me out. I think we like justice if we *agree* with it. But if we are in the wrong and get punished in some way; if justice is served 'against us'; we don't always like that, do we? No one loves a parking ticket, even if it is justly served!

Isn't it wonderful to know that in God we have a holy judge who can't be cajoled by clever arguments into thinking differently about what He knows to be right? No one can convince Him not to love us or forgive us or act justly towards us. No one can change Him from being a God who is slow to anger and abounding in love (Neh. 9:31). Isn't that great? For me, that is the most wonderful justice there is.

Optional further reading
Psalm 33:1–5; 2 Thessalonians 1:5–7

The Lord **is righteous**

I have been fascinated by a high profile court case unfolding in the news recently. The families involved waited years for justice to be done and for the truth to be known. They described their wait as a 'constant fight', but one they had no intention of surrendering. It is true that as humans, we have an inbuilt need for a righteous end to injustice, because we are made in the image of God. God is a God not of fairness, but of justice.

Isaiah 61:8 begins, 'For I the LORD, love justice.' We are left in no doubt about how God feels here. He is clear. The word 'justice' is taken from the Latin *iustitia* meaning 'righteousness and equity'. Psalm 11:7 tells us something key to help us understand more about *why* God loves justice. It says, 'For the LORD is righteous, He loves justice.' The reason God loves justice is because He *embodies* it. He *is* righteousness. He *is* justice. Verse 4 of today's passage explains this characteristic of God more fully: 'He is the Rock, his works are perfect, and all his ways are just. A faithful God who does no wrong, upright and just is he.'

I love the fact that God is described as the Rock. He won't move away. He won't crumble or fall. His decisions and actions are perfect because He is just. At the end of Isaiah 61:8 we read more of this permanent Rock-like nature of God: 'In my faithfulness I will reward my people and make an everlasting covenant with them.' If we build our decisions and our lives on God, we will not be shaken. All God's ways are just.

Deuteronomy 32:1–10

'all his ways are just.' (v4)

For prayer and reflection

Father, thank You that You are righteous and holy. Thank You that Your promises are everlasting. Amen.

Known as **blessed**

**Galatians
3:13–14,26–29**

'So in Christ
Jesus you are all
children of God
through faith' (v26)

When people say, 'I have been blessed by God!', they are often referring to a material comfort, or some kind of success or healing. But what does it mean to be known as a *people* whom the Lord has blessed? What would it look like for your family, community or church to have that kind of reputation?

If we look back at God's blessing of Abraham in Genesis 12:3 we read God's promise: 'in you all the families of the earth will be blessed.' That is quite a statement. It is one thing to *receive* a blessing but quite another to *carry* a blessing for others. I think that is a challenge for all of us. But it is also an encouragement. It is a reminder that we are blessed to be a blessing – our blessing carries the DNA of being passed on.

We all want to live under the blessing of God, don't we? We ask Him to bless our homes, our work and our food. When we receive good things from Him we say we are being blessed. But in Galatians 3:13–14 we read: 'Christ redeemed us from the curse of the law by becoming a curse for us... in order that the blessing given to Abraham might come to the Gentiles through Christ Jesus.'

So when Isaiah prophesies that God's descendants will be known among the nations and refers to their offspring among the peoples as being blessed, he was talking about them also being *free*; free from restraint, free from oppression, free from foreign gods and free from curses. We have a God who longs to bless us. His plans are to prosper us and not to harm us; to give us hope and a future (Jer. 29:11).

**For prayer and
reflection**

**Lord, teach me
to count my
blessings and
name them before
You. Help me
recognise the
value of each of
them in my life.
Amen.**

Delighting **greatly**

O ther children were present, but I only had eyes for my daughter. It was as though no one else was taking part in the sports day at all. All my focus and attention was on her. In every race, hers were the eyes I fixed on. After each event, she was the one I sought out.

When we 'delight greatly in the LORD' (Isa. 61:10) there is no room for other gods. When we tell our souls to rejoice in God, we are truly focused on Him and Him alone. Our gaze is not elsewhere. Our eyes are fixed on Him, the author and perfecter of our faith (Heb. 12:2). These wonderful words about 'delighting greatly' in Isaiah 61:10 are echoed by the ones Mary sings in today's passage, having been visited by the Angel Gabriel. She sings, 'My soul glorifies the Lord and my spirit rejoices in God my Saviour, for he has been mindful of the humble state of his servant. From now on all generations will call me blessed, for the Mighty One has done great things for me – holy is his name.'

From the inside out, this soul and spirit rejoicing is what stabilises us. It is what enables us to be called people of blessing. When we set the Lord before us, as Psalm 16:9 encourages us to do, we are told that we 'will not be shaken'. Not only this, but our hearts will be glad and our bodies will rest secure. Focusing on God fully brings joy, and also deep peace and security.

In what areas have you felt shaken and wobbly? Do you think it might be because you are not 'setting the LORD' before you? In what ways could you 'delight yourself in God' more?

Luke 1:46–56

'my spirit rejoices in God my Saviour' (v47)

For prayer and reflection

Lord, thank You that You are worth delighting in. Thank You that You always satisfy our hunger and our thirst. Amen.

More than **wedding guests**

....

Hosea 2:16–23

....

'you will call me
"my husband"; you
will no longer call
me "my master".'
(v16)

Whenever a wedding invitation arrives at our house, almost the first thought that appears in my mind is, 'What am I going to wear?' So often when we go to a celebration or special occasion, our minds will turn to our clothing or to the preparations for that event.

Isaiah 61:10 talks about the Messiah as the bridegroom – one of Jesus' self-chosen titles for Himself (see also Matt. 9:14–15; Mark 2:18–20).

In the Old Testament we often find passages where the nation of Israel is expressed as being God's bride. For example, in today's passage, Hosea writes down God's voice to Israel saying, 'I will betroth you to me for ever; I will betroth you in righteousness and justice, in love and compassion' (vv19–20).

So what does it mean to be Jesus' bride? When Jesus was on earth He paid a dowry for us on the cross with His own blood. We belong to Him. He has promised to come a second time and take us to Him. Ephesians 5:25–27 explains, 'Husbands, love your wives, just as Christ loved the church and gave himself up for her to make her holy, cleansing her by the washing with water through the word, and to present her to himself as a radiant church, without stain or wrinkle or any other blemish, but holy and blameless.'

A good bridegroom is always attentive to his bride. He can hear her whisper and her cry. He knows her heart and wants to have closeness and intimacy with her.

In what ways do you need to be reminded that You belong to Jesus? Are you ready for Him to return? Are there areas of your life where You are not acting like His bride?

....

For prayer and reflection

....

Jesus, thank You for inviting me to Your table; for the invitation for the Church to call You 'husband' instead of 'master'. Amen.

Seasonality

had kept those seeds for years. Lost in the darkest corner of the garage, I had totally forgotten about them. When I held the packet, I noticed that the 'use by' date had passed some five years earlier! But I still planted them. I wanted to see if life could be found in those tiny, brown, dried-up tear drops. And sure enough, I was not disappointed. Miraculously, those seeds did come to life – and flowered, too.

Sometimes, God keeps us in the dark earth like a seed for a long period of time. It can feel as though we are buried but not blessed. We can feel in the dark and without purpose. But God reveals to us in verse 8 that He is in charge of our seasons of growth. Seeds grow silently, secretly, slowly and steadily. In Genesis 8:22 God promised Noah after the flood, 'As long as the earth endures, seedtime and harvest, cold and heat, summer and winter, day and night will never cease.'

Seasonality is something we can struggle with. We want to be permanently fruiting and blossoming, don't we? But God has promised us seasons. This means we may need to be content to look a bit bare and barren for some periods whilst God is building our roots system, or pruning some unnecessary branches. We may need to be content with no apparent growth until the seasons change. God is in charge of the secret growth that even we can't see.

What does the garden of your life look like at the moment? What season would you describe yourself in and why? Do you think God has hidden anything in You that is yet to sprout and flourish?

1 Corinthians 3:1–8

'The one who plants and the one who waters have one purpose' (v8)

For prayer and reflection

Thank You, God, for choosing to plant me in the right places. Grow me at Your pace, according to Your plans. Amen.

WEEKEND

You are sovereign

For reflection: 2 Samuel 7:1–11

'The LORD himself will establish a house for you' (v11)

In this world of constant social media output and regular reports of bad news that is generated across the globe, it is wonderful to think about the truth behind the word 'sovereign'. However bad things may get, our God is *still* on the throne. Isaiah 61 starts and finishes with that name for God – the 'Sovereign Lord'.

In my life, I am so glad God is sovereign. When I don't understand, I am glad God is sovereign.

When I grieve, I am glad God is sovereign. When I doubt, I am glad God is sovereign. When I am low, I am glad God is sovereign. When I make poor decisions, I am glad God is sovereign.

When I hurt others or bring shame on myself, I am glad God is sovereign. When I fear the future or regret the past, I am glad God is sovereign. When I am angry and hurting, I am glad God is sovereign. When I am happy and liable to forget His goodness, I am glad God is sovereign.

In our passage today we see how God gave David rest. Thank Him today that as Your sovereign God He will establish 'a house' for you also.

Optional further reading

Habakkuk 3; Jeremiah 32:17–23

Order form

5 Easy Ways To Order

1. Phone in your credit card order: **01252 784700** (Mon–Fri, 9.30am – 5pm)
2. Visit our online store at **www.cwr.org.uk/store**
3. Send this form together with your payment to: **CWR, Waverley Abbey House, Waverley Lane, Farnham, Surrey GU9 8EP**
4. Visit a Christian bookshop
5. For Australia and New Zealand visit KI Entertainment **www.cwr4u.net.au**

For a list of our National Distributors, who supply countries outside the UK, visit **www.cwr.org.uk/distributors**

Your Details (required for orders and donations)

Full Name:	CWR ID No. (if known):
Home Address:	
	Postcode:
Telephone No. (for queries):	Email:

Publications

TITLE	QTY	PRICE	TOTAL
		Total Publications	

UK P&P: up to £24.99 = **£2.99**; £25.00 and over = **FREE**

Elsewhere P&P: up to £10 = **£4.95**; £10.01 – £50 = **£6.95**; £50.01 – £99.99 = **£10**; £100 and over = **£30**

Total Publications and P&P (please allow 14 days for delivery)	**A**	

All CWR adult Bible reading notes are also available in **eBook** and **email subscription** format. Visit **www.cwr.org.uk** for further information.

Subscriptions* (non direct debit)

	QTY	PRICE (including P&P)			TOTAL
		UK	Europe	Elsewhere	
Every Day with Jesus (1yr, 6 issues)		£15.95	£19.95		
Large Print *Every Day with Jesus* (1yr, 6 issues)		£15.95	£19.95	Please contact nearest National Distributor or CWR direct	
Inspiring Women Every Day (1yr, 6 issues)		£15.95	£19.95		
Life Every Day (Jeff Lucas) (1yr, 6 issues)		£15.95	£19.95		
Mettle: 15–18s (1yr, 3 issues)		£14.50	£16.60		
YP's: 11–14s (1yr, 6 issues)		£15.95	£19.95		
Topz: 7–11s (1yr, 6 issues)		£15.95	£19.95		
Cover to Cover Every Day	Email subscription only, to order visit online store.				
Total Subscriptions (subscription prices already include postage and packing)				**B**	

Please circle which issue you would like your subscription to commence from:

JAN/FEB   MAR/APR   MAY/JUN   JUL/AUG   SEP/OCT   NOV/DEC   *Mettle* **JAN–APR   MAY–AUG   SEP–DEC**

*Only use this section for subscriptions paid for by credit/debit card or cheque. For Direct Debit subscriptions see overleaf.

We promise to never share your details with other charities. By giving us your personal information, you agree that we may use this to send you information about the ministry of CWR. If you do not want to receive further information by post, please tick here. ☐

Continued overleaf >>

<< See previous page for start of order form

Payment Details

☐ I enclose a cheque/PO made payable to CWR for the amount of: £ _____

☐ Please charge my credit/debit card.

Cardholder's Name (in BLOCK CAPITALS) _____

Card No. ☐☐☐☐ ☐☐☐☐ ☐☐☐☐ ☐☐☐☐

Expires End ☐☐ ☐☐   Security Code ☐☐☐

Gift to CWR   ☐ Please send me an acknowledgement of my gift   **C** [_____]

Gift Aid (your home address required, see overleaf)

giftaid it I am a UK taxpayer and want CWR to reclaim the tax on all my donations for the four years prior to this year **and on** all donations I make from the date of this Gift Aid declaration until further notice.*

Taxpayer's Full Name (in BLOCK CAPITALS) _____

Signature _____ **Date** _____

* I am a UK taxpayer and understand that if I pay less Income Tax and/or Capital Gains Tax than the amount of Gift Aid claimed on all my donations in that tax year it is my responsibility to pay any difference.

GRAND TOTAL (Total of A, B & C) [_____]

Subscriptions by Direct Debit (UK bank account holders only)

One-year subscriptions cost £15.95 (except *Mettle*: £14.50) and include UK delivery. Please tick relevant boxes and fill in the form below.

☐ *Every Day with Jesus* (1yr, 6 issues)
☐ Large Print *Every Day with Jesus* (1yr, 6 issues)
☐ *Inspiring Women Every Day* (1yr, 6 issues)
☐ *Life Every Day* (Jeff Lucas) (1yr, 6 issues)

☐ *Mettle*: 15–18s (1yr, 3 issues)
☐ *YP's*: 11–14s (1yr, 6 issues)
☐ *Topz*: 7–11s (1yr, 6 issues)

Issue to commence from
☐ Jan/Feb ☐ Jul/Aug   *Mettle* ☐ Jan–Apr
☐ Mar/Apr ☐ Sep/Oct   ☐ May–Aug
☐ May/Jun ☐ Nov/Dec   ☐ Sep–Dec

CWR Instruction to your Bank or Building Society to pay by Direct Debit

Please fill in the form and send to: CWR, Waverley Abbey House, Waverley Lane, Farnham, Surrey GU9 8EP

Name and full postal address of your Bank or Building Society

To: The Manager   Bank/Building Society

Address _____

Postcode _____

Name(s) of Account Holder(s) _____

Branch Sort Code ☐☐ ☐☐ ☐☐

Bank/Building Society Account Number ☐☐☐☐☐☐☐☐

Originator's Identification Number

| 4 | 2 | 0 | 4 | 8 | 7 |

Reference

Instruction to your Bank or Building Society

Please pay CWR Direct Debits from the account detailed in this Instruction subject to the safeguards assured by the Direct Debit Guarantee. I understand that this Instruction may remain with CWR and, if so, details will be passed electronically to my Bank/Building Society.

Signature(s) _____

Date _____

Banks and Building Societies may not accept Direct Debit Instructions for some types of account